贝多芬

Heroes and Role Models | Non-Fiction Series

Copyright © 2022 by Level Learning, INC. and Washington Yu Ying PCS™
Original and Edited Text Copyright © 2022 by Washington Yu Ying PCS™

All rights reserved. No part of this book in whole or part may be reproduced without written permission from the publisher.

Published by Level Learning, INC.

Content Contributors:
Washington Yu Ying PCS™
Level Learning - Ya-Ching Chang

Illustrations by: Josh Taira

Leveling classification based on Level Learning standard. For full description, visit www.levellearning.com

ISBN 978-1-64040-010-8
Simplified Chinese Edition

About Level Learning:
Level Learning provides a literacy focused curriculum specifically designed for K-12 Chinese as a Second Language classrooms. Our program offers 20 levels of specific and detailed objectives, leveled texts and passages, mastery-based online assessment, and analytics to enable data-driven instruction. Level Learning reading curriculum for both literature and informational text emphasize grammar and comprehension skills to help teachers develop confident and independent Chinese language readers. The non-fiction series of books are specifically designed to support our informational text course based on multiple national standards. To learn more about our entire offering, visit www.levellearning.com.

About Washington Yu Ying PCS™:
Washington Yu Ying PCS is a Mandarin English dual language immersion International Baccalaureate (IB) World school. Yu Ying's mission is to inspire and prepare young people to create a better world by challenging them to reach their full potential in a nurturing Chinese/English educational environment. Yu Ying's comprehensive IB, dual immersion curriculum equips students with global competencies for success in the real world. As a leader in immersion education, Yu Ying is determined to advance Chinese language programs and global citizenry education by helping other schools create and strengthen their Chinese programs. For more information, email: products@washingtonyuying.org

贝多芬生于1770年。他是在德国出生的。

贝多芬的爷爷和爸爸都是音乐家。因此,他小时候就常常和爸爸学习音乐。

贝多芬非常喜欢音乐。他也进步得非常快。

贝多芬小时候就常常参加音乐表演。大家都很喜欢他的表演。

长大以后，贝多芬到维也纳学习音乐。在那里，有许多有名的音乐家。

在维也纳,贝多芬经常参加音乐表演。他也学习作曲。

可是后来,贝多芬的耳朵听不清楚了。慢慢地,他听不见声音,也听不见音乐了。

虽然听不见,贝多芬还是**努力**地作曲。

贝多芬写了九首有名的交响曲。他也成为了一位有名的作曲家。

Glossary

	Pinyin	English Definition
德国	dé guó	Germany
出生	chū shēng	born
音乐家	yīn yuè jiā	musician
学习	xué xí	to learn
音乐	yīn yuè	music
进步	jìn bù	to improve
参加	cān jiā	to participate
表演	biǎo yǎn	performance
维也纳	wéi yě nà	Vienna
有名	yǒu míng	famous
作曲	zuò qǔ	to compose
听	tīng	to listen, to hear
清楚	qīng chu	clear
声音	shēng yīn	sound
努力	nǔ lì	work hard
交响曲	jiāo xiǎng qǔ	symphony